GLENISE BORTHWICK enlisted in ... armed with a teaching certificate ... Diploma in Education from Glasgow University and a degree in English and Communications. She joined the English Department at Vale of Leven Academy in West Dunbartonshire, where she quickly learned that having a sense of humour is sometimes the only thing that gets teachers and pupils through the school day. She became a full time trade union convener for teachers in West Dunbartonshire, then moved to Edinburgh and joined the General Teaching Council for Scotland, initially as their Investigating Officer, and then Communications Officer. She is now Head of Communications with the Council and editor-in-chief of *Teaching Scotland*.

BOB DEWAR was born in Edinburgh at an early age. Sixteen years later he was published nationally. He worked in D.C. Thomson's studio where, among other things, he ghosted Dennis the Menace. After going freelance, he did political and social commentary for *The Scotsman* newspaper. He has illustrated books for many publishers including the Children's and English Speaking Departments of Oxford University Press, and for Fife Educational Social Development. His work has also appeared in *The Times*, *The Herald*, *Scottish Field* and The Scotch Malt Whisky Society newsletter and on its Members Room ceiling. He has had exhibitions in Lucca, Italy, in Glasgow and in Edinburgh and had caricatures hanging in the House of Commons. He is now a lot older than 16 and is married to the novelist Isla Dewar, with two sons and an absurdly friendly big golden retriever. Bob has no idea how this friendliness happened, since he tends toward grumpiness.

Top Tips FOR Teachers

Tips by GLENISE BORTHWICK

Illustrations by BOB DEWAR

Luath Press Limited

EDINBURGH

www.luath.co.uk

First published 2008

In association with

ISBN (10): 1-906307-20-2
ISBN (13) : 978-1-906307-20-2

The paper used in printing this product is recyclable. It is elemental
chlorine free (ECF) and manufactured from sustainable wood pulp
forests. This paper and its manufacture are approved by the
National Association of Paper Merchants (NAPM), working towards a
more sustainable future.

Printed and bound by Thomson Litho, East Kilbride

Typeset in Century and Futura by 3btype.com

Illustrations by Bob Dewar

This book is dedicated to the charity Education Action, and to all teachers who give freely of their time, experience and hearts to help their international colleagues and pupils in war-torn areas of the world where education offers the only real pathway to freedom.

All royalties generated from sales of this book will go towards realising these aims.

Introduction

Teaching is not an easy career option and I know all too well that there are days when a teacher's patience is tried to the limit. These tips are written to support teachers. Stepping back and just remembering the warmth and fun of the good days gets us all through the more testing moments. Trials are common to all of us, a collective humour that we laugh at because we've all been there, we all know the experiences.

As editor of *Teaching Scotland*, the magazine for teachers registered with General Teaching Council for Scotland, I was aware that there had to be a balance in the tips between humour, wisdom and practicality. The laughter comes from a mutual respect and a process of learning and understanding nurtured between teacher and pupils over time. No one expected those first tips published in *Teaching Scotland* to be so successful, but the response was amazing and people began to write in offering suggestions or simply saying how helpful they had found the advice. *Top Tips for Teachers* was born out of the idea that teachers could not only share their experiences, but also could help a charity make a difference to education across the world.

Read these tips in the spirit in which they are intended – down-to-earth advice from someone who still passionately believes that teachers can make a real difference to a child's future and that education matters.

They like you more than you realise

Teachers come quite far down the pecking order for pupils, trailing badly in the list of preferences that includes mobile phones, DVDs, computer games and chicken nuggets. They may make your life difficult, but you are more important to them than any of these items. Although you do not bleep, flicker or teach to catchy music, you point the way to their future. Bask in the warmth of this thought.

It's great that some are keen, but don't ignore the others

Some pupils, in their sheer enthusiasm to answer a question, will get over-excited and throw their arms in the air, jump up and down behind their desk, or even resort to shouting out your name to drown out all other attempts in the room. There are other pupils who will not enter this display of attention-seeking as it does not match their cool image. Choose many pupils to make sure everyone gets a turn and only reward over-exuberance occasionally.

Get different skills to work together

As you get to know your pupils you will work to their strengths. You'll know the good leaders, the good contributors who will lead discussion and keep ideas on track, the artists who will turn your walls into the Louvre and the team members who will carry the cup home at the end of the season. Different talents work together in a classroom and school. Get to know your pupils and get Picasso working with Beckham.

Accept the rich tapestry of smells

It is a fact that some pupils smell nicer than others. Wet weather causes the steaming pupil syndrome. There is little you can do other than let them dry off. Pupils leaving Physical Education also have their particular odour as they compete against each other to smell perfumed. This is the rich tapestry of smells associated with teaching. The smell you must immediately act on is that of dog poo on an unsuspecting pupil's shoes. An afternoon in your classroom with the offending odour of Rover can ruin your lessons.

Develop an inner self

Learn to temper your language and always be the professional in the classroom. You can think to yourself 'How can they be so stupid?' or 'How can they make such a mess of this?' but you must never say it. You will develop the inner you and the outer you – the one that screams loudly but silently on the inside, and the one that smiles gently on the outside.

You can be overshadowed by the weather

The slightest change in the weather will gain immediate attention from your pupils over anything you say or do in the classroom. Just expect, on occasion, to be upstaged by heavy rain or a strong gust of wind. Snow will totally eclipse your lesson as your pupils sniff early closure in the air.

PARIS JENNINGS
JADE SMITH
CHANTELL MUNRO
ZORBA
MAXIMILIAN HAPSBURG
ATTILA ROBERTSON
LORENZO THE
MAGNIFICENT...
(JUST KIDDING)

There's not much in a name

Don't let a name influence what you think about a pupil. If you have a Wayne in the football team don't expect him to take trophies for you. Likewise if you have Chanterelle in the room don't expect her to have heard of the mushroom she has been named after. Pupils have strange names at times. It is not their fault, but you will somehow have to get over it. Names come in batches, and there will always be a clutch of pupils coming through named after the latest hot pop star. Kylie has now worked its way through and out of the secondary schools, as has Britney with a late surge of Jades and Chantelles on their way. Be grateful for the ones you can spell. Pupils are landed with names they neither wanted nor like. You will need to read it out on the register each day, so don't make it a stick to beat the poor pupil with, nor a joke everyone tires of.

The tap, tap, tapping of the fidgets

Classes will always have fidgets. Pupils will find something to play with, or to fold into a dozen pieces. They like to fidget when you are busy teaching for all you're worth at the front of the class. Had they taken their knitting to school, the really good fidgets would be producing eight pullovers a week and taking orders. Just make sure they fidget with their own pencil cases and paperwork and not with school property. Try to quieten the really noisy fidgets who get over-absorbed in their activity.

Don't play behavioural chess

Constant poor behaviour will drive you crazy. You have to deal with it before it drives you under. Try not to let it keep you awake at night as you scheme and create strategies trying to outwit their next move. The truth is they don't have a next move or even a plan, and you've been up all night pacing the bedroom in your furry slippers playing behavioural chess against an imaginary opponent. You'll go in ready to battle the next day and the opposition is sitting, doing their work. Pupils are fickle.

Watch out for signs of sneaky texting

Despite the school policy that mobile phones are switched off, many pupils will attempt to text during a lesson. It is a challenge to many, an addiction to others. You will know the signs: the beeps and the heads down. This will cause you stress and affect how much you can tolerate in the classroom. Make sure they know the rule and enforce it. As far as your own phone is concerned, make sure it is switched off and if it rings because you have forgotten to switch it off, that it has a tune of some credibility. Prepare to defend your choice of *The Muppets* theme tune to exacting, trendy pupils.

As a teacher you are in a high performance job, which will need energy and well-being. Your diet will help you through this. So think broccoli, think fruit and think healthy. You need to look bright and fresh, as very often you will be the only one exhibiting these features in the classroom. You have to carry pupils who may be attempting the curriculum on fuel made up of pizza and artificial flavours through the day, so keep hydrated and wean yourself off the caffeine.

Eat right

Fine-tune your body language

Do not over-gesture. Do not cause a draft by flapping your hands about to emphasise a point. But equally do not be so unexpressive that your entire body looks as though you've just had a massive Botox injection. Don't look like a rabbit in the headlights nor lie back on your chair with feet up on the desk. Be yourself, but look and act professional. Pupils react to how you look and act.

Keep a bad day in perspective

There are days when your sanity will fight for life in your classroom. Grab the lifejacket that reads 'not every day will be like this' and head for the shore.

Would you get to the point already?

Accuracy, brevity and clarity are a two way street. Don't beat your pupils into mental submission by drowning them with long explanations, anecdotes and repetition. Get to the point as quickly as you can without meandering down lanes and pathways of thought.

No two parents are the same

Don't be shocked when you meet parents. There will be surprises from aging rockers to body-pierced and tattooed mothers. They are still caring parents even if they overdose on hair gel and body art. Enjoy diversity and don't stare. You are neither there to judge the parents nor to get the phone number of their tattoo artist as you hanker after that discreet but tasteful tattoo you've always wanted.

Be selective about collecting materials

Don't turn into a collector just for the sake of it. Think useful; think necessary. Resist the urge to cut out and copy everything. There is a finite number of times you can use those carefully kept pictures of Vikings, so be selective and don't spend too much time building up your collection. Better to have one premier lesson than several from the substitution bench. Remember to swap and share.

Let them assume you're deaf

All pupils consider that teachers go deaf when they are not looking directly at them. It's part of classroom folklore. They also consider that teachers have blind spots and that there are safe areas of the classroom to misbehave and have private conversations. They forget that teachers are the masters of multi-tasking. This ignorance can be useful to you. Use it well.

Keep those sick bags handy

School trips can bring on binge eating by pupils who come armed with large plastic containers filled with everything from cold chicken legs to a mosaic of pizza slices. They come ready for a siege on the bus. Inevitably, many pupils will need a good number of toilet and fresh air stops as you try to turn them back into a decent colour from the various shades of green that they turn into. They will need your sympathy as the bus hurtles down the motorway and the driver informs you that there will be no impromptu stops on the hard shoulder. Bags and wet ones are the order of the day for keeping your charges clean and dry. Should you become ill, expect the pupils to deny any responsibility for you. The caring attitude to travel sickness is not reciprocal. You need to make sure you are the invincible one. Take your own bag for accidents.

Always hit save

Computers decide to shut down or plead ignorance when it comes to saving a very important document you have spent some time on. Your finger takes on a life of its own when the computer asks if you want to save changes and it hits no.

This has two effects on you: one is to make you cease to breathe for at least seven minutes when you realise the error of your ways; the other is for you to press every key you can in the forlorn hope that it will appear by magic on your screen. It must be there somewhere, so you end up in the bowels of computerland where you discover a whole new world of singing icons and page numbering tips but, sadly, no document. Save, save, save and don't let the technology get to you.

Be aware of staffroom mug politics

Staffrooms are areas of fashion and image. Your mug should have a witty saying, thoughtful picture or be at the cutting edge of the most recent Ikea design. It says something about you, so watch out for allowing your image to slip into a chipped or cracked mug. Tension can be caused when two mugs of the same design appear. Watch out for this. Some mugs become abandoned and remain by the sink for years, their owners long retired. These are often used for visitors. Rinse the dust out of them.

Be constructive, not destructive

You must do a number of things to keep parents away from your classroom door with a complaint. Do not be disparaging about a pupil's personal appearance, their home, the wallpaper they covered their jotters with (which was lovingly placed on the lounge walls at home), their choice of holiday or the family's inability to control their pets, which are working their way through your pupil's jotters. Think how your snide remark can be interpreted and remember an angry parent will want you to justify your comments.

Reenergise during the breaks

Take some time during the day at school to relax and keep calm. It's very tempting to work through your breaks and lunchtime, but you will tire and burn out by the end of the day. Lunchtime should be for re-energising yourself. You can use the time to get out of the building or take part in some gentle exercise. Some teachers use stretching exercises at their desk to ease stress. If you partake in this particular activity make sure you do not have an audience. Otherwise, some thoughtful pupils will report you to the school office because they think you're having mental difficulties.

Positive reinforcement works better than yelling

You will always come across the pupils who need constant nudges to keep them on the educational pathway. Use the nudges of repetition and reinforcement rather than those of shouting, growling and glaring.

Never take sides in a battle between students

You cannot get involved in arguments that are for five- to fourteen-year-old pupils. Much as you may have an opinion, it belongs to you. If pupils realise they can bring you into their open warfare, they will use you to legitimise their comments and also use you to referee their battles. You are in charge of the classroom, not the adjudicator of disputes.

You definitely have a weird idiosyncracy

If you think you do not have a mannerism, then think again! Pupils will pick up on the arm waving, the fiddling with the watch, quiet humming or pen chewing. Things you never thought you did are amplified in the classroom arena. Pupils do not do this on purpose. It's just that they sometimes have to look at you for fifty minutes or a day at a time and after a while, these movements become obvious and strangely irritating.

Be thankful for the staffroom

Teaching was never going to be the career with long lunches and champagne receptions. Make the most of staffroom lunches and in-service scones and cups of tea. Join the Hobnob club and appreciate the joys of a biscuit.

Stay one step ahead of the pranksters

Some areas of the school are traps for the unsuspecting pupil and teacher. Banisters on stairways are favourites for pupils to spit on. Watch out for others having to wipe their hands furiously to remove the offending fluid. Watch where you put your hands and what you lean against. Every day is a new challenge for some pupils – just be aware.

Your embarrassing moments will go down in history

Do not indulge in the grand gesture in front of your pupils, such as acting out a battle scene or a romantic part of a poem. If things go wrong you will enter the folklore of the school for a very long time. If you do not want to be immortal for an outrageous lesson or comment, keep your gestures to a minimum.

Pupils can get used to a broken record

There is no point starting your lesson unless everyone is listening. You will wear out your energy levels, and create stress, by repeating yourself over and over as each pupil finishes their own conversation. They quickly catch on to the fact that they can listen to you when they are ready, as they know you will repeat instructions. Say it once, write it up or have it on the top of the worksheet and that's it.

Take a few tips on amateur film-making

If you are making a film with the class, take some instruction and some hints on getting the best from your pupils. It's harder than it looks. Pupils can get switched off very quickly if you film your feet and only your voice is heard shouting instructions into a mike only inches under your nose. Over-exuberance on tracking and panning shots can make your pupils feel sick as they watch your artful movie-making. They like to see themselves on film, so think about getting them in focus rather than making your trailer for a BAFTA nomination.

Ease back into school after summer

Pupils enjoy being back after a holiday to catch up and get updated on holiday romances and escapades. But getting them back into the swing of things can be difficult, especially as you keep looking at that picture of yourself lazing on the Greek beach which you insist on keeping on your desk to punish yourself. Recognise that you are all starting off from the same point: wanting to be elsewhere. You are now on the first lap of the teaching Grand Prix. Take a big deep breath and ease down slowly on the accelerator.

Eager pupils can be like clinging koala bears

Younger pupils like to get your attention without waiting a turn. They will pull your clothes, tap your arm, drape themselves over your desk or demand eye contact. Get them into the habit of raising a hand. That way you can move around the room without a pupil attached to you. Watch out for raised hands and respond to these when you can. Watch out for the half raised hand – that shows there's been a time lapse in getting your attention.

Be sensitive to separated parents

Some parents wish to avoid each other at a parents' evening for all sorts of reasons. Some are recently divorced, and find being in the same geographical location as a previous partner too traumatic. Agree to meet them apart and factor in possible delays to your timings. Your pupil needs all three of you, so talk about the pupil and keep out of domestic problems. If you get asked, 'Did he bring that blonde with him?' plead ignorance.

Be gentle with snoozers

There are ways of dealing with a pupil who falls asleep in the classroom. One of them is not to suddenly shout at him. You'll frighten the other half dozen who were just about to join him. A gentle word in their ear is enough, then find out the reason – a late night, an early rise, your lesson? Keep the room well ventilated and don't allow outside jackets to remain on. If you see anyone nodding off, ask him or her a question to keep them alert or even conscious.

You can't win the pencil war

Pencils and the trauma of pencil borrowing will play a large part in your teaching career. You can go down the road of marking 'your' pencils, of buying easily identifiable pencils and pens, of counting them in, out and around the classroom. But ask yourself this question: 'Is it better to make them responsible for having their own pencils or will you always give them yours?' Pupils like pencils and they will like your pencils no matter how dog-eared they are or how ghastly they look. Many have the red pens straight out of the bookies, others the pencils from Ikea. As long as they are able to write, be pleased. Good luck in the pencil wars.

Use real names in the classroom

Don't encourage the use of nicknames in class. Cheesy, Shorty and Rebel are fine for the playground. Keep to the name on your register.

They'll pull the wool over the covering teacher's eyes

If you are going to be out of school and have to leave lessons for a colleague to deliver, make sure you leave them a copy of the lesson and do not sellotape it onto the desk. Pupils understand this method of passing on information and will remove it or change your lessons. They will convince the covering teacher that they were to have a DVD that day. Do not leave anything in chalk, as your lesson will turn into a collection of rude words on the board as pupils rub out letters. They can be very inventive.

One day you'll have your own staffroom chair

Staffroom politics start off and finish with comfort and position. Teachers like to sit in the same chair in the staffroom. Some have had 'their' chair for many years. One day you too will have 'your' chair and be equally possessive about it. It is a rite of passage. Just don't get into the habit of claiming a chair by throwing your jumper onto it. The staffroom is not the beach, so don't go early to stake a claim.

Graffiti

Graffiti is not the new art form

Watch out for graffiti in the classroom. It's like a rash and will spread if you do not control it. Keep clearing it up. Do not weaken to the idea that graffiti is the new art. Your room is not a gallery. Self expression should be kept within the confines of the curriculum.

Support parents but don't get too close

Parents' meetings are not about traumatising the pupil, the teacher or the parent. They are supportive and informative meetings. No matter how big or how scary a parent or guardian may look or act, they need the truth and help for their charges. Don't overindulge a parent; keep to the allotted time. Waiting parents get grumpy and you can get off to a bad start. Watch out for the not-uncommon parent's need to share personal problems with you. Alarm bells should ring and you should not go there, regardless of how interesting you find the conversation.

Make a difference and don't count down the days to escape

Throughout your career you will attend retirement parties and leaving events as teachers make it to the barrier and make their escape to sunnier climes and afternoons with a bottle of red. You will, in time, be handed a spade that will allow you to dig your part of the escape tunnel. In the meantime, remember that you are needed by an awful lot of children and have a big part to play for society, so don't spend your time thinking 'escape' just yet! Don't be caught in the staffroom counting off the days until the end of term.

NATIONAL
SPORT
IN SCHOOLS

Monitor pupils who participate in the Toilet Olympics

Keep a record of pupils who wish to go to the toilet. This is a national sport in schools. Pupils often agree to meet with a friend or just use the time to escape from you and your lesson. Do not be party to their antics. Keep a list of whom you let out and when. This is good for any instances of vandalism or if you have to show a pupil proof that they are making this a habit.

You are the master of all classroom decisions

Your life as a teacher is all about making decisions every day and every hour. You will decide who is doing what, where and when, what your pupils need, what you need and what everyone else needs to allow you to concentrate. A bell will ring to allow you to refuel, ready to make more decisions between the custard creams and the Hobnobs in the staffroom. As the day wears on you will become tired, so that by the time you get home you will find that really simple choices become huge undertakings. That is because you are all 'decided out'. There is nothing wrong with you, so don't worry if you find yourself in the supermarket unable to make a simple decision between a carrot and a leek.

Develop a flock mentality

Some trips will involve changes on public transport. If you are venturing onto trains and buses and planes, count everyone on and off. Use your flock mentality by keeping everyone near to you. Nothing can scare a teacher more than the tube doors closing and a pupil waving goodbye as you shoot off to Piccadilly Circus minus one. Keep their mobile phone numbers close by and let them know your strategy entitled 'If you get separated from the group'. Losing a pupil even for a few moments is never an option and will seriously affect your stress levels.

Listen to both sides of the story

No matter how angry you are, always let your pupils tell you their version of events. What you see going wrong isn't always the full story. Even the worst pupil in the room can sometimes be the innocent party, although all your instincts will not be in their favour. You hold the scales of justice in your hands. Use them fairly and don't let stress and exhaustion colour the truth.

Never let a bad student know your true feelings

Remember that embarrassing your pupils should not be part of your classroom tool box, no matter how appropriate you may think it would be. Try not to blame, shame or hurt feelings. Encourage, support and praise where you can and keep any mean thoughts well under wraps.

Preview all DVDs

Watching a DVD should be the easiest lesson in the world to organise. Everyone sits facing the screen, the blinds are down and anticipation is high. You put the DVD in and press play. Your nightmare begins as you realise that:

a   You should have checked it.

b   It's too late to do anything about it. You have trusted your pupil to bring in dancing penguins, but what you've ended up with is the brother of said pupil carrying out his karaoke performance, unsuitably clothed with intermittent shots of cartoon penguins.

Let this be a painful lesson: check everything before viewing in the classroom.

Avoid competing over who brings the best food to parties

Staffrooms have events to mark retirements and birthdays and holidays and babies, the whole range of life-changing experiences. Early on, you will have a signature dish you will bring. Some people do not cook and do not have such a dish. Allow them to bring coleslaw from the supermarket and don't challenge them to be more inventive. It's a time for fun, relaxation and breaking the diet, not a battle of the chefs.

Practise care in social chats with parents

Be wary of social chat with parents and never say how like his father your pupil is. Nowadays there are too many options in relationships, and the person in front of you may not be the real father. You may be the cause of an argument and some real hurt that the parents take home. Think carefully and keep to the curriculum.

Teachers need nap time

Napping is not age related. You need quiet me time when you get home after a long day of lining up pupils, collecting jotters, counting in worksheets, stopping disagreements, seeking out pencils, emphasising points, detailing and repeating and breaking up arguments. Your brain has been a racetrack all day so now is your time for a pit stop. Put your feet up, have a snack, a herbal tea or something stronger, and hug the dog or your significant other. Be inventive and don't feel guilty.

Discourage 'desk blogging'

Pupils like to partake in 'desk blogging' as often as possible. One pupil will begin the conversation scrawled in pen on a desk and others will respond and embellish it with artwork. Before you run out of clean desks, stop the conversations and wage war on the scribbles. Think of ways to put their creative energies to better use.

Pupils have no concept of time

It's always a good idea to have a clock in your classroom. Pupils have no real concept of time during a lesson and sometimes really do think the lesson is nearly over when you've only been in full flow for a matter of minutes. Time can seem like an eternity to your charges and they will constantly ask you what time it is or how long is left. You can just point to your clock and let them blame time itself for dragging – but remember to check on the clock at the end of classes as winding it forward may be tempting to some of your pupils.

Don't be a fashion victim. Pupils just live in wait for you to wear that little pink number again or the corduroy jacket that has come out for one last term. Be sensible in what you wear. T-shirts with statements are asking for trouble and the school polo shirt doesn't look good on everyone.

Beware what you wear

Try not to get songs stuck in your head

Music is infectious and you will end up humming a tune that you picked up simply by passing a pupil humming it in the corridor. It will stay with you all day and you will seriously doubt your sanity when you find yourself indulging in your *Dirty Dancing* routine in the book store. Stay professional, stress free and fight the urge.

Plan for delays

Make time during every lesson for handing out and collecting papers, getting started and summing up. Teaching is not a quick sprint. It's more like a marathon and you have to outlast everyone in the classroom. Take your time and make sure you have everyone in the race with you before you jog into the curriculum.

Keep an eye on the staffroom notice boards

Teachers don't read notices on staffroom walls. Unless your staffroom wall is updated regularly, information that goes on it will be lost in a time warp. Watch out for the staff party pictures, which get sneaked onto notice boards. You may not look your best photographed under harsh lights when you were obviously trying to focus after a small sherry, but swallow your pride and enter into the spirit of staffroom community.

Where they sit on a bus is a big deal, so don't mess with it

Seating arrangements on a school bus can be tricky. Best leave the pupils to decide on their own seats unless, of course, you find you have to send a peace-keeping force up to the back seats just once too often. It's a rite of passage thing. Older pupils lay claim to the back seats because that's where they perceive the action to be. Remember that the destination is the point of the trip, so don't get exhausted with the seat wars before you even get there.

Stick to your lessons right up to holidays

Pupils are programmed to go into relaxed mode at the very sniff of a festival or holiday. They will convince you that it's time to make decorations for the classroom or to let them watch a DVD. For your own sanity, keep the curriculum going as long as possible and keep the treat for the very last day. They will use your weaker colleagues, who have given in and have a classroom of paper bunnies depicting Easter, to bait you. They will bemoan your lack of festive spirit and indulge in tantrums and huffs. Don't weaken. After all, you can only watch *Grease* so many times.

Your disorganisation is a waste of time

Always try to set a good example to your pupils by being organised. They get to know very quickly that they can waste time at the start of the lesson while you rummage in your desk and cupboards looking for jotters, worksheets and books. They will entertain themselves while you retrace your steps trying to work out where you left a mark sheet or lesson plan. Remember to rise with dignity if you are under your desk in search of the elusive paperwork, and watch out for the drawer that you've left open. Pupils will ask to see the bruise!

You may think you're Bruce Willis, but...

Pupils are obsessed with celebrity. It is just a fact of this generation. You may think that you have the look of Beyoncé or Bruce Willis about you. Do not share this with your pupils unless you are prepared to:

a   Be deeply hurt.

b   Realise the truth that you don't look at all like your celebrity.

c   Be mocked and teased mercilessly about it forevermore.

Keep your ideas and hopes to yourself. That way you can continue to believe in them and hold your (lookalike) head high in the corridor.

If there are ink stains, they will know you're a teacher

Teachers like to use fine markers. It's always a real giveaway in a pub when your shirt has an ink stain in the pocket. Try not to lose the lid of your pen and remember to put it back on before if goes in your pocket. Very soon you could find your entire wardrobe 'teacher marked'.

Don't be mistaken for a squirrel

Rather than make camp in the storeroom looking at all the worksheets you've encountered at each school you've taught in, ask your colleagues what worked and what has value. You will become overwhelmed as you look around the riches of support materials. Less is more, so select and dip in. Carry only what you need and don't be found in the corridor with large black bags of worksheets and folders you're spiriting into the classroom like a squirrel.

But teacher, he did it first!

Pupils tell on each other. They cannot help it. They cannot keep a secret and will throw their classmates to you as an offering for you to back off them. They have very little loyalty to each other if there is public humiliation in the air or street cred is in danger of being damaged.

For some unknown reason, pupils will sabotage your plants

It's always a nice idea to have a plant in your classroom as it gives the room that 'cared for' look. Sadly, some pupils have a need to pull off leaves and what was your pride and joy can become an unsightly stick by the end of the first term. They don't have a personal vendetta against foliage; it's just too tempting a challenge for them. Don't take revenge by introducing hostile plants with spikes, or you'll find yourself removing spikes and thorns from overreacting pupils and explaining yourself to parents.

Sometimes TV is more important

Do not get too disappointed if your lesson fails to compete against an event of great magnitude from the TV the night before. Have a quick chat about what was so engaging and then move on to the lesson. Let some bubbles out of the bottle to let the lesson settle; keep the fizz for the playground.

Don't trust the glazed and nodding stare

Pupils have become very skilled at making you think they are interested and listening to you. They look as if they are paying attention but are quite unconscious to everything going on around them. Some call it a wakeful sleep – they can look at you and may even be nodding or smiling, but mentally they are still in their beds or at the concert from the night before. This is not personal to you, the teacher. The problem is school-wide, as lessons get in the way of pupils' preferred activities.

Give your mug a good cleaning before it grows legs

From time to time, take your mug home for a thorough clean unless you are using it to grow cultures for a lesson. Teachers are notorious for a rinse and go mentality to crockery. Unless you want your school to be mentioned on the six o'clock news as the source of an unpleasant outbreak of unfriendly bacteria, get into a healthy relationship with your mug and introduce it to your dishwasher.

You'll bump into students outside of class

Expect at some point in your career to meet an ex-pupil in a social setting you least expect. You will recognise your pupil only when she is handing over the cream you have on prescription from the chemist for that irritating rash, or you suddenly recognise the helpful voice in the changing room when you are standing there in your Bridget Jones knickers trying to squeeze into your size sixteen top.

Students can't get enough of those loopy, swirly, bold and crazy *fonts*

Pupils like to use the complete range of fonts available on their computers when typing up work. From century gothic to dingbats you will see them all. They will make your life miserable as they work their way through the ornate, the bold and the plain ridiculous. As long as they get the work completed you can wean them off the more absurd ones.

There's no reason to strain your voice

Don't shout. Either speak normally or take your comment to the individual or groups you want to attract or inform. Your voice is necessary for your job, so train your pupils to pay attention and keep your volume for the football at the weekend. Warm up your voice before you get to the classroom either with your favourite tunes on the way to work or by practising your scales in the shower. Pupils have no mercy when you lose your voice and will not be motivated if you only have a squeak.

A clever way to avoid the rollercoasters

School trips will test you to your limit. Do not consider it beneath you to hold coats and bags whilst pupils and more adventurous staff members hang upside down on gravity-defying rides, screaming their heads off. You are safely on the ground keeping your dignity and your dinner down.

Pupils' priorities

Pupils have a set of priorities when they are out of school. Homework is on the list but not in the first fifteen of 'must do' things. Homework comes after hair gel, chocolate, trash TV and devotion to calories. Be pleased and content that the world of knowledge is part of the agenda for pupils be it somewhere between nail painting and crisp eating. Once the more pleasurable activities that feed the body are in place for your pupils they'll get round to the mental activity.

Check all worksheets before they're handed out

As if teaching was not stressful enough, machines do their very best to cause you to move ever closer to that scream in the bookstore. Photocopiers have a capacity to lie about the number of sheets they print out. You press ten; they give you eight and two blank sheets neatly hidden in the pile you have just given out to the class. Pupils do not like sharing and disagreements over ownership break out across the room. A blank sheet given to a pupil very quickly converts into the latest MiG fighter plane that comes screaming across the room towards you or lends itself to a life drawing of a member of your class. Check sheets before they go out and try not to kick the photocopier next time you have those sharp-toed shoes on.

Go green

Recycle in your classroom. Have a bin for cans and one for paper. Make a lesson out of it. Draw the line at having to go into your bin at the end of the day with your rubber gloves to separate the apple cores from the chewing gum. You can do your bit without having to handle the paper hanky full of chewed pizza remains.

Expect mixed feelings about displaying student work

Suggesting to your pupils that you will display their work on the wall in full public view brings out the best and worst in them. Some will be inspired to produce work that will be viewed with awe by others. Some pupils will be appalled that their work will be on show at all. Listen to pleas about displayed art and work with the volunteers. Crucially, watch out for sabotage! Jealousy can raise its head when artwork is compared; additions and comments can appear on the work that can offend or surprise.

There are more options than right or wrong

Don't always have only one correct answer in mind. If someone is close but not quite there give praise. If pupils realise that they can only be right or wrong, those who will only be in the vicinity of the answer will give up. Let them know you appreciate the journey and not just the arrival of an answer.

Let them have headphones... sometimes

Music on the bus is best played directly into the ears of your charges. If you want a shared moment of communal music make sure it's something that will neither fray your nerves nor make an enemy of the bus driver.

Keep your private life private, especially on the web

Pupils have an insatiable thirst for details about your private life. Keep this to yourself unless you want it to come back and haunt you. The wonderful world of Bebo and Facebook can make your life just a Google away for some pupils. Be careful what you publish on the web and any information you give out about yourself. Pupils talk to each other and the information held by one becomes the property of all.

Have patience while they ramble on

Teaching is about patience. Sometimes it will take your pupils a while to explain something to you and get to the point. Sometimes there will be no point whatsoever. The fact is that you will have to listen to this and share a moment with them. Find your caring side.

For some inexplicable reason, students think they're anonymous on tape

Using a tape recorder in the class to record a group discussion or individuals' experiences can be a good idea, but be warned that pupils have this insatiable desire to swear into a microphone or make as many suggestive comments as possible to embarrass the teacher. They really do believe they become anonymous on tape. Try to get them over the rude remarks, and get used to using the tape recorder as a classroom tool.

Network like mad

Teachers are often allowed out to meet other teachers as part of in-service and Continuing Professional Development. Make the most of the time and swap ideas, notes and good lessons. Network like mad. Talk to the volunteers and not the conscripts who don't want to be there.

For a big mess, call in the expert

Pupils of all ages need a paper hanky at some point either to mop up spills and accidents or to howl into when their romance of three days has ended. When the accident becomes heavy duty, leave it to a professional as you are not trained nor equipped to deal with excessive body fluids. Remember to remain cool and in control when a crisis takes place, as pupils will take their lead from you. If you yell and fall over there will be an unattractive heap on the floor as the more dramatic will swoon and drop with you.

Students like to steal pins

Items that can be removed from your classroom walls will be removed. Blutack, drawing pins and sellotape are all removed with a stealth and a secrecy that will astound you. Posters and papers will remain suspended until the pupils have left the room, and will then gently waft down once the offenders are off the premises. Use as little blu-tack as possible to make it less attractive for stealing and push drawing pins well into the pin board to at least present a challenge to would-be thieves. You may well love your coloured pins for the notice board, but so will your pupils. Try a stapler instead.

You are very old fashioned; deal with it

As far as your pupils are concerned you are from another era, another mindset and often another planet. Be yourself and rejoice in the very difference between you.

Hormones run high

Like it or not, your pupils will fall in and out of love on a regular basis. This behaviour is not age-restricted. Whilst you are fine-tuning your lesson at the front of the room they will be eying each other up and down, ready to make a smart move at the interval. Hormones are your enemy. You will not win against them. Keep the window open to cool the ardour and always keep the lesson on track. Do not get involved in relationship counselling no matter how much you have an opinion. These relationships will often move onto the second stage very quickly: rejection. Prepare for tears and turmoil.

You can't always get what you want

There will be days when you will have to change a lesson because something hasn't quite worked out the way you want or pupils haven't responded in the manner that you expected. This happens no matter how experienced you are. Classes can have group moods, individuals have 'off days' and external events will impact on your lesson. Always have another lesson ready to substitute. No good performer goes on stage with one joke, regardless of the audience. Learn to read the mood of your class but remember to keep to the curriculum and your own forecasts and plans too.

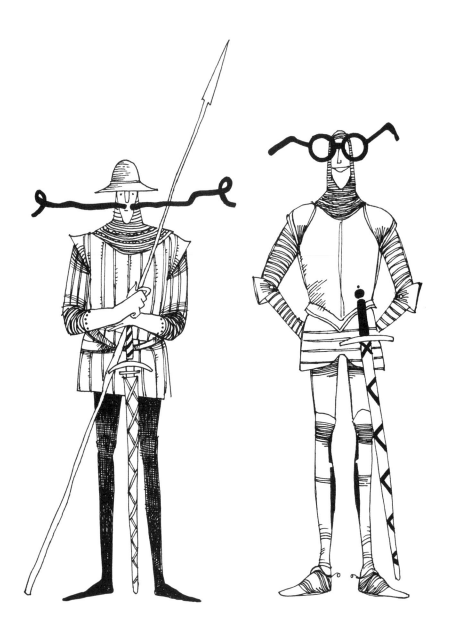

Don't let the crime scene go cold

Keep your worksheets clean and graffiti-clear by checking them as they come back from the class. Images you have carefully chosen for your worksheet can have artistic embellishments added and words changed so that your sheets are verging on pornographic. There's no use getting angry next time you go to use them and they have football scores, details of classroom romances and modern art adorned across them. You will never find out who caused the damage no matter how good your detective skills are. Crime scenes go cold the longer the case goes on, so be on top of damage and vandalism.

Manage your photocopier rage

Photocopiers know when you are stressed or in a hurry. They will refuse to copy, jam the paper and run out of toner. This is not personal, despite every sign pointing to the contrary. They do not have human emotions, so shouting, physically assaulting and threatening their electricity source will have no effect on anything but your blood pressure. Don't leave copying to the last moment and do not get photocopier rage.

Some days you're super, some days you're not

Teachers are like changing room mirrors to pupils. Some days your pupils will see you as the super duper teacher, your knickers on the outside of your trousers, your cape flying in the wind. Other days you are the irritating blob there to make their life a misery with dollops of pain and mental agony. The truth is you are both. That's teaching!

Take a little lesson from the Rolling Stones

Keeping a lesson alive after having taught it many times is not easy. Remember it may be the fiftieth time for you but it's the first time for your pupils. You can use the same jokes and the same support material. Take a look at the old rock bands such as the Rolling Stones. The same material with new sets, lighting, and a dash of charisma can lead to 'come back' lessons over and over again.

You can't hide under the duvet

Remember that hiding under the duvet and not wanting to go to school is something that will happen to you from time to time. You share this in common with your pupils. It's like everything else. Once you get there it's not so bad and it will take one small success to make you remember why you became a teacher, and why you make the effort to get up, dressed and out to work. You will have these thoughts on dark, cold mornings when you have a difficult lesson ahead of you. Throw yourself into the challenge the day will bring and remember that your duvet will still be there for you to crawl back under should the day not go according to plan.

Give credence to the know-it-all older teachers

The sage in the corner of the staffroom may well moan and groan, announce the number of days until the next holiday or tut at your enthusiasm as you arrive with huge piles of support materials and visual aids. He's seen it all, heard it all, got 20 years notched up of teacher stress and experience. Listen in on his grumbles and learn from the experience. It will help you survive once your own early enthusiasm has been tempered and will allow you to match the notches.

Keep their eyes open and eyes forward

Teachers are often accused of disturbing their pupils' natural school-time sleep cycles. Students can be triggered off to sleep by certain words in the teacher's vocabulary such as work, think, revise or effort. It will be your duty to keep them awake so they can engage with the curriculum. Eyes open and eyes front for everyone!

Watch out for face-pickers

It is a fact of classroom life that pupils of all ages like to squeeze, prod and pick at scabs and spots – often on each other. This is part of growing up. Don't get involved other than when an offending part of a pupil has been left on the desk on their departure. Either you will have to remove it or the next occupant of the desk will bring it your attention. Be strong and don't look too close.

They're not just irritating to spite you

Some pupils have really bad mannerisms that they have nurtured over the years and have taken time to hone into extremely irritating habits that can drive the teacher up the wall. These have not been developed just to annoy you. Try not to focus on them. Avoid the temptation to throw yourself across the desk and grab the pencil that has been tapped just once too often.

Be careful what you search for

You now have the world at your feet in terms of information through the Internet. When you are surfing in your ever-lasting quest for more inform-ation for your lessons and ideas for the curriculum, be careful what sites you venture into. It can be very difficult explaining to the IT people at school why that woman in the red dress is dancing about on the screen and refuses to be deleted and why exactly you were on so many sites looking for a Swedish partner in your attempts to find a school for pen friends for your class. Think where you are going – records are kept!

Monitor group discussion

Pupils have an amazing ability to keep to the topic of their group discussion whilst you are within earshot and go back to analysing the primary seven romances when you are not. You will need strategies to keep them on track. Try timing discussions, watching them at different intervals whether you can hear them or not, or asking them searching questions. Remember the Pinkerton's Detective Agency motto: 'The eye that never sleeps.' Just don't get too carried away with your plotting and scheming to keep within earshot, because it will scare the pupils.

Get them engaged

Getting the whole class involved is always good teaching. Ask questions and keep everyone's attention alert. You may think that everyone is on board; but do not be surprised when an enthusiastic hand flies up only to ask a question that has little or no relevance to your subject. Your lesson will not quite reach everyone. You will seldom connect with all the brains in the room at the same time.

Retain your dignity in an embarrassing moment

You must at all costs keep your dignity in the classroom. Top class acts, when they are performing in front of an audience, rehearse and prepare often, with flair and style. If you trip over a bag, reverse into a small pupil or drop an entire pile of jotters to great applause, try not to swear however quietly you do so. Pupils can lip read. Move on with the lesson and nurse your embarrassment and dignity in the staffroom where there will be comfort and understanding.

Don't share food

Swap recipes with your pupils if you think they have an especially appealing lunchbox, but do not trade. The memory of swapping that really nice looking biscuit with the unknown diabetic will linger long in your memory as you watch the ambulance leave the building.

Everyone cries, but try to keep it in

Everyone cries at some time and often over the oddest thing. Don't always expect it to be girls either. The trick is not to join in, so if someone is upset try to find out why. Don't end up borrowing their hanky for a good howl. A sudden picture of the deceased pet pulled out of a pocket can catch you unawares and bring back sudden painful memories of your own Cuddles or Tiddles. Stay strong.

Always stay alert

It is your duty as a teacher to look motivated, keen and enthusiastic. If you look sleepy, bored or just not interested then your pupils will take their lead from you.

Feel warm in the thought that you can feel what you want inside but not reflect those thoughts on the outside. The general always has to enthuse the foot soldiers, so play your part in the classroom.

When tempers flare, address the problem with a cool down time

Temper will overtake all sense some days, often for a good reason. If you feel you are getting close to the edge of your sanity, don't go for the big confrontation in the classroom. Take the pupil out for some cooling down time. The issue will get worse if the whole issue explodes in front of the whole class. Your blood pressure will suffer, and the lesson will be ruined. Really serious issues just have to be dealt with there and then and the rest of the class has to see that certain behaviours cannot be tolerated. Try not to take the whole issue home with you, going over what could have been done to resolve or even prevent it in your head. Bad situations just happen because a cocktail of conditions have taken place. Learn from it and move on. Take 'you' home and leave 'them' behind.

Say what you mean, and mean what you say

Never say, 'This is your last chance'. In your heart of hearts you'll know it won't be and that you'll end up giving your pupil another pencil or another evening for her homework. Pupils become deaf and immune to repetitive comments. Both they know, and you know, that your options are limited. What you have to do is make the limited options work. When you say no, mean no. Pupils have powers of pleading and persuading second to none. Do not enter into negotiations. You will not win. Once you become known to react positively to a quivering lip, a downward look or painful whine you will be lost.

Even social time needs a few guidelines

End of term is a time for the teacher to get to know their pupils in a more social setting, be that riding around a local park on a bike or watching a DVD in your classroom, where you can cry together at the sad ending. But spending social time with pupils can be like living with the neighbours from hell. Have rules and standards even in this more social setting to stop the over-friendly pupil becoming disruptive.

You're somewhat of a mascot

You will be surprised how much loyalty your pupils have to you as 'their teacher'. You will become like a pet and they will defend you against other pupils who are not 'yours'. Pupils seldom show that they actually like you, as it is not cool to do so. Just as pupils get used to seats and classrooms, they get used to you too.

Education Action

Education Action has been helping some of the poorest people in the world since 1923. Founded as World University Service [WUS] we have a distinguished history. However, with the help of our many supporters, we will also have a distinguished future.

We focus on education in former war-torn countries and with refugees from war in the UK. The countries we work in – Sierra Leone, Uganda, Sudan, Angola and Palestine among others – have fragile education systems. All too few children get to go to school and, for those who do get to school, the quality of education is often not good enough.

So we have a particular focus on quality. It's no good getting children to school if they leave illiterate and innumerate. We innovate by trying out new approaches to providing education that will help change the lives of millions of children and their families.

If you want to help – and we need money for the work we do – please visit our website at and find out how to donate.

Thank you for your support.

www.education-action.org